A Walk in Victoria's Secret

Southern Messenger Poets

DAVE SMITH, *Series Editor*

A WALK IN
VICTORIA'S
SECRET

POEMS

KATE DANIELS

LOUISIANA STATE UNIVERSITY PRESS ⟩|⟨ BATON ROUGE

Published by Louisiana State University Press
Copyright © 2010 by Kate Daniels
All rights reserved
Manufactured in the United States of America
LSU Press Paperback Original
First printing

DESIGNER: Mandy McDonald Scallan
TYPEFACE: Adobe Caslon Pro
PRINTER AND BINDER: McNaughton & Gunn, Inc.

Library of Congress Cataloging-in-Publication Data
Daniels, Kate, 1953–
    A walk in Victoria's secret : poems / Kate Daniels.
    p. cm.
    "LSU Press Paperback Original."
    Includes bibliographical references.
    ISBN 978-0-8071-3706-2 (pbk. : alk. paper)
    I. Title.
    PS3554.A56363604 2010
    811'.54—dc22

                        2010032846

Grateful acknowledgment is made to the editors of the following publications, in which the poems listed first appeared: *America:* "The Hatching"; *American Poetry Review:* "Photos by William Christenberry"; *Blackbird,* "The Pedicure"; *Cortland Review:* "Doc"; *Five Points:* "Crowns," "The Figure Eight," "The Polack," "Shampoo Girl," "When I Was the Muse," and "The Writer"; *Image:* "A History of Hair," "Scar," "Sheet: A Psychology of Hatred"; *Louisiana Literature:* "Cigarettes and Matches"; *New Labor Forum,* "Autobiography of a White Girl Raised in the South"; *Northwest Poetry Review:* "Peep Show"; *Oxford American:* "Autobiography of a White Girl Raised in the South"; *Poetry Daily:* "When I Was the Muse"; *Solo:* "The Divorce"; *storySouth:* "Homage to Calvin Spotswood," "Crowns," "The Polack," and "Photo by William Christenberry"; *Vanderbilt Review:* "Louisiana, Late Summer"; *Verse Daily:* "When I Was the Muse"; *Women's Review of Books:* "A Walk in Victoria's Secret."

"Homage to Calvin Spotswood" also appeared in *Best American Poetry 2008.*
"Late Apology to Doris Haskins" first appeared in *Under the Rock Umbrella* (2006).
"Scar" also appeared in *Bearing the Mystery: Twenty Years of Image* (2009).
"Self-Portrait with Religion and Poetry" first appeared in *Crazed by the Sun: Poems of Ecstasy* (2008).
"A Walk in Victoria's Secret" also appeared in *Best American Poetry 2010.*

for

Mark Jarman
Philip Levine
& Dave Smith

my tellers of stories of "deep delight"

Having, then, formed the project of describing the habitual state of my soul in the strangest position in which a mortal could ever find himself, I saw no simpler and surer way to carry out this enterprise than to keep a faithful record of my solitary walks and of the reveries which fill them when I leave my head entirely free and let my ideas follow their bent without resistance or constraint.

—J.-J. Rousseau, *The Reveries of the Solitary Walker*

CONTENTS

1

A WALK IN VICTORIA'S SECRET

> If an infant could speak, he would no doubt pronounce the act of sucking at his mother's
> breast by far the most important in his life.
>   —S. FREUD

In an hour, I'll be lying on the worn-out, mauve-colored couch
in the 30th month of my psychoanalysis, free associating
on the tables of brassieres in Victoria's Secret, & how I love
to wander there, touching the puce-colored slips of silky polyester,
fingering the diminutive, twinned flags of cups and straps, imagining
the privileged, frivolous lives they'll enter. Gently, my analyst might press me
to recall the name of my mother's mother—*Victoria!*—and I'll make
the connection, proceeding to ruminate on the hard, closed facts
of her private life. I'll speak of her breasts (which I never saw) the image
incongruous among this merchandise: the bustiers gratuitous with champagne-
colored lace, the hot pink, underwired, front-clasping bras, the gelatin-enhanced
heavyweighted cups for women craving more . . .

Then something will turn me petulant—the over-familiar, dusty-smelling
odor of the analytic couch, or an unidentified inflection in my analyst's voice—
and I'll emerge from the guilty fantasy, and back up into the familiar
territory of the conscious mind, condemning the girly-girliness
of Victoria's Secret, and professing my feminist admiration
for the Phallic Mother who charges through the world as empowered
as Demeter. Still, I can't resist the lure of the totally objectified
un-phallic mother who exists in a creaturely daze, solely for the pleasure
of the yearning Other . . . Thus, I drag my hands through the palpable eros
of Victoria's Secret, re-visioning, no doubt, the brief paradise
of my mother's "breast"—a series of rubber nipples affixed to the end
of a boiled glass bottle, and rigidly administered on an hourly schedule.

⌒⊷

Any history of my own life would start there, of course, and proceed
through brutal weaning: overnight, the nipple was retired, and the hard rim
of a metal cup replaced it in my mouth. In certain moods, recumbent
on the couch, I can feel the murky, ancient outlines of that yearning infant,

her mouth working the bad calculus of early withdrawal, her undeveloped
mind all in a whirl, unable to satisfy the desire to suck . . .

I love smelly, sweaty breasts bound in practical spandex to contract the orb's
circumference and inhibit unbalancing jiggling in order to swing,
unimpeded, the number nine club on the eighteenth hole,
three under par, in the previously closed-to-women National Open . . .
And then there's the miracle of lactating breasts with their stretched nipples
and swollen globes of succulent flesh, the skin thinned at the sides,
raising the blue veins to the surface so it looks like a map.
I love breasts fastened into nursing bras with their flip-down
cups, facilitating a jutting-out as hilarious as coarse characters
in a Vegas strip show. I love the historical breasts of the milk nurse
who took up the noblewoman's babe and suckled it for wages.
And the furtively, thrust-through breasts, warming the iron bars
of the debtor's prison where the inmate took his comfort
from his mother or his wife. I love proletarian/redneck/sensible shoes/24-7/
workaday breasts, cheerfully spewing full-course meals or midnight snacks,
or fast food, drive-thru repasts while speeding down the interstate.
I love the milky nu-nu stuffed in the mouth to plug up the titty baby's untimely yowl.

Last night, I watched my sons on the O-line of the football field,
so distant in their grown-up bodies, so far from mother's milk.
To remind them now of the meals they made of me would mortify
and unman them, so I keep that silence. Afterwards, I embraced them
in their helmets and their pads, and leaned hard into the rank,
erotic fragrance they emitted, yearning to return to our early years together,
when I was hardly more to them than a universe of approaching odor,
a twin-hulled, human spaceship rocketing across a galaxy
with my bursting, squirting cargo of warm, sweet milk . . .

I loved the smell inside my nursing bra. I used to dip my face inside,
and breathe, and pull away, feeling drunk solidarity with my hungry baby.

I loved the sodden *thunk* of soaked nursing pads flung to the floor.

I loved the oily, thin taste of my own milk.

I loved my husband's mouth, in the dark, relieving the pressure.

I loved the mounting. My baby mounting his objects of desire,
and making them run with milk, sucking out the cream,
raising the heat and falling back, drunk and gluttonous,
almost post-coital, on the sweaty, smelly pillow of my flesh.

Now that it's all over, now that my breasts are diminished and dried out
and will never run with milk again—

Now that my nipples are like those of a grammar-school virgin,
and look like raisins desiccated past their prime—

Now that the specter of cancer of the breast is statistically more
than a distant possibility—
Now that two empty bottles in the window above my writing desk,
once filled and refilled with Holman's Dairy milk, permanently
remind me of my former glory and gleam straight through
with absence, I need only touch my chest to imagine—

Now I walk through the radiance of Victoria's Secret, drunk with the ghostly,
concave images of all those robust breasts, waiting to be suckled and cupped.

⌒▰

In her barely literate way, my mother's mother must have meditated
on the dual mysteries of every woman's breasts that Freud, in his genius,
almost ruined: the sweet delight of a baby's nursing, and the harder edges
of the pleasure delivered by a moaning lover's sucking mouth.
Far back in the previous century, I have conjured Victoria. I can
see her after supper, leaning over the dishpan in the kitchen sink, her mind
blessedly free of psychoanalysis. She pumps a basin full of cold, clear water,
and opens the front of her gingham dress, and lifts her beauties

from the thick white bindings of her homemade bra.
Leaning awkwardly, she dips them down and dabs them with a roughened,
dripping cloth. All day, her man has labored in the fields. In a corner
of their room, his dungarees crouch in crusted piles of stench as he falls, exhausted
on their bed. Even so, tunneling at the very edge of sleep, he moves towards her
for a tiny sip of sweetness, a sugary lozenge of buttery candy, he pulls into his mouth.
Now energy pulses him distantly, back in time, until he becomes
his very own, newborn baby. All's delightfully confused. Who is he now?
The child he put inside her belly two years back? Or his ancient, infant self
at ease upon the paradise of his mother's breast? And she, the phoenix nesting
on her bed of self-extinction, is sucked away deliciously. She's an object,
for the moment, experienced as subject: the breaking yolk of warmth between her legs,
the untidy buzzing rush of hormones in her head, the milk rising and rising,
breaking so exquisitely the unanalyzable mystery of flesh.

Autobiography of a White Girl Raised in the South

From the day I was born, I began to learn my lessons.
 —LILLIAN SMITH, *Killers of the Dream*

In any self-portrait from the '50s, you'd have to see the me
that was not me: the black girl trudging along the side of the road
while I whizzed past in my daddy's car. Or the not-me
girl in the bushes, peeing, while her mama kept watch
and I relieved myself inside, daintily, in the sparkling facilities
of the Southside Esso, labeled WHITES ONLY. All those
water fountains I drank from unthinkingly, the lunch counters
where I disdained my lunch—she was there on the wooden benches
bleached by sun out back of the store, or squatting on a curb
sipping from a Mason jar of tepid water lugged from home,
or eating her sandwiches of homemade biscuits and a smear of fat.

From the beginning, then, there were always two: me and not-me.
The one I was, white and skinny, straight brown hair. And the one
I wasn't, but could've been—that black or brown girl, hair coarser
than mine, eyes darker, skin gleamier and smooth, free of freckles.
I didn't even know where she lived, only saw her in public
when she stepped up on my granny's back porch with a paper bag
of okra, accompanying her mama, selling turnips and tomatoes,
or her daddy, with his tools, come to sharpen the knives.
Then, we eyed each other, I recall, hands behind our backs,
faces solemn and shy, our hair plaited, mine in one long, compliant
tail—but hers in a dozen marvelous sprouts, each tied off
with colored twine. Now, I think it's odd, cruel even,
I never shook her hand, showed off a toy, or asked her out
to my special place in my grandmother's yard,
the powdery patch of gray dust beneath the cherry tree,
where blossoms plopped down in tiny clouds of air and color.
There, cross-legged, knee to knee, we might've touched
each other and satisfied our terrible curiosity—
whether she, in fact, was just like me, and I, like her.
For a moment, sheltered by the blossoms of a flowering tree,
the universe might have seemed to us like the garden

it once was—various and multitudinous, aswarm
with rich textures, interesting odors, a wide palette of color and hue.

Instead, I kept my head down and watched her toes, bare and curled
in the powdery gray-brown dust, and felt envy for her going free
of shoes, and had no idea of the images that might be passing
through her mind. Then I heard my granny's much-loved voice,
calling from the porch, to come away and go inside. She sent away
the not-me's daddy without a sale, and chastised me throughout our lunch
for what she called "familiarity." And through the back screen door,
I saw the not-me girl, walking away behind her daddy, not
looking back, and I heard his voice, querulous, too, chastising
her, as well, for something bad, whatever it was we almost did
but didn't, finally, dare to do.

DOC

His last name is lost now, misfiled
in the archives of my personal history—
but I've never forgotten him,
that cute, black, pre-med sophomore
from Lafayette, Louisiana, who wore
aviator glasses and tattered khakis,
so intent on becoming a surgeon
his roommates called him Doc.
I remember he lived on the ground
floor of a garden apartment with sliding
doors and vertical blinds that one of us
must have locked and twirled shut
to ensure our privacy. Grilled T-bones
decorated our plates, and while we cut and chewed,
I regaled him with an anecdote of poor Ted Roethke,
so psychotic in his mania, he believed
he was a lion. "Bring me a steak,"
he had said to the waiter. "Don't cook it. Just
bring it." And for some reason, both of us
laughed. Then I quoted the phrase I had always loved,
"Suddenly I knew how to enter the life of everything around me."

In the silence after that, the end of the evening
approached quickly. I could taste the beef grease
on my lips, and feel its heaviness in my gut.
The hot, arousing smell of cooked flesh
filled the air between us. And before I realized it,
Doc was leaning toward me, his eyes limpid
behind the huge lenses of his glasses,
his mouth relaxed, his hands soft.
I could find nothing in his face
to frighten me, and something old
inside was punctured and started to empty,
draining itself like a ruptured boil.
And though that felt like a healing, poison
still poured out, dampening the space

where Doc and I now stood, close enough
to smell each other . . .

No one who could possibly care
knew we were there, alone, reverberating
inside the prison house of history,
longing to touch each other
free from context. One kiss
would transform me to the n——r-lover
my old friends determined I'd become.
And Doc would be pilloried beside me
for impersonating the race-traitor
a black man loving a white girl
was called back then . . .
All it would take to free ourselves
from the old narratives and continuous
loop reruns of our national nightmare
was six more inches and a slight elevation
of my quivering chin. The lower halves
of our bodies were already touching,
and Doc's arms looped loosely, encompassing
my ass . . .
            But when I touched him,
when I raised my hands and fit them
on the smooth brown bulges
of his muscled biceps, the automatic ignition
of cultural reproduction switched on,
and the feeling that filled me then
was something like a rush of wings
unfurling and souring the room
with a musty odor . . . For a few hours,
Doc and I had cleared the air
of racial difference and met
each other in a rare element, debrided
of color. Now, as our bodies clamored
for the culmination, clouds of old history
reverse-fumigated the room, and something

as ominous and unambiguously black
as Poe's raven, croaking its warning,
Nevermore, infected the room. Thus,
I tensed and flexed before I turned my cheek
to make a landing pad for the silken slide
of Doc's sweet lips on my schoolgirl's skin.
And then, without looking again
into his beautiful eyes, I picked up
the cage I had brought, and turned to go.
I fitted the quilted cover down over the silver bars,
and buckled it close. I listened to darkness quiet
instantaneously the creature trapped inside.
Then I bore it away with me, swinging
in my hands, and walked home alone,
through the darkened, shuttered streets.

THE FIGURE EIGHT

The swan's path is a calm infinity in Boston Common's
public pond. In it, closing back on itself after every turn,
I see the fragile image of my younger brother
in the years before his marriage failed, the rented farmhouse
south of Richmond he shared with friends, laborers
like him at DuPont Chemical. In the evenings,
their gray uniforms dark with sweat, their hair flattened into oily mats,
they squat together on the worn wood steps to smoke
a few joints and guzzle cheap beers, tossing the empties
towards the edge of the wood. They ignore the shattering.
A few minutes of silence before the alcohol kicks in,
its spidery fingers scrambling gratefully in their guts.
And then they're bitching themselves into a state of restlessness—
they've finished with the niggers and the god-damned democratic
president, dispensed with the northerners' spiel
on collective bargaining. They're onto women now—
what cunts they are, how all they want is to take you
for a ride. Pissed at the child support somebody's
paying, the abortion another one's wife refused to have.
And without even speaking, they rise and walk down
into the meadow, their cigarettes gleaming weakly in last light,
to the place where the old car rests, a junker someone finagled
for $85 and a lid of dope. An Oldsmobile or something that
glamorous, from the 1950s, once turquoise and sleekly desirable,
Elvis blaring from the perforated speakers in either door,
a shapely car hop leaning down to latch a silver tray of fries
and shakes on the rim of the driver's window . . .
One of them hotwires it alive and my brother slides in, grinning,
lit now, somebody at last, both hands gripping the wheel, and takes off
around the meadow as if—this time—he might really be going somewhere.
His buddies howl when the car stalls out in a deep rut
and then roars to life again, blue smoke breaking
through the back of the engine. The car is whining and popping
with breakage, its back end swinging back and forth, the way
a wounded dog keeps going, homing for its master. The wheels
are straining, like that, trying to moving forward,

but he's just going around and around, around
in the mud-stiff ruts, somewhere there in the dark cab,
his head cloudy, his mind set on nothing but the figure eight
he's making in the mud, inscribing it deep in the earth
so when God looks down He'll see the sign for infinity,
the same shape of the neat path the swan swims
in the pond at the public gardens where I sit, years away
several lives distant, a universe removed, my hands
shaking, my mouth dry, writing down the words of this poem.

THE PEDICURE

It was a birthday gift from my husband who remembered,
I suspect, the luscious, toe-sucking days of our early lust.
Now, a hard decade into parenting and home ownership,
those tentacular extensions of our mutual pleasure
had surrendered their erotic glow, and grown mundane
as garden stones displaced beneath the blankets of our bed.
On the divergent altars of comfort and high fashion,
I had sacrificed their beauty in the tiny coffins
of ancient, archless sneakers and size six, four-inch
slingback heels, the ones my husband loved to watch me in,
tottering swaybacked across the restaurant floor, a little tight
from the wine, my ass compensating for the extra height
by sashaying its heart-shaped halves more heavily than usual.

Perhaps it was for him, then, hoping to revive that long neglected
garden of our early love, that I ascended a seat as elevated
as a throne, on the morning of my 50th birthday,
at Womanly Illusions: A Day Spa for Modern Women. Gingerly,
I thrust my feet into the waiting hands (so warm and soft!)
of the white-garbed girl who crouched beneath me—a gesture
so unconsciously imperious I cringed inside to do it. Behind my eyes
flickered tiny images of my mother on her knees, scrubbing floors
in empty offices, evenings after work for extra pay. Whole legions
of my family crowded in behind her: some of them also on their knees
in torn jeans and dirty aprons, in the garish colors of the easy-launder
polyester uniforms of the service class. Some of them were cudgeled
by the bastards who pocketed the profits of their labors. And some
had turned to cudgeling, themselves, whipping without satisfaction
or self-understanding those they claimed to love. Yet here I was
with my sympathy for the workers, my love of Marx, my hatred
and fear of the bourgeoisie, the robber barons, the planter class,
all kings and queens, the Ferdinand and Imelda Marcoses, the Richard
Nixons and George Bushes of the world. Here I was, *swooning*
(not too strong a word) at the pricey ministrations directed at my feet.

Despite myself, I let go of the past and succumbed to pleasure.
I could feel my consciousness slipping. Then the gate was torn
from its hinges and the workers surged through. Suddenly,
they were lying down on the job! Stripping off their coveralls
and safety goggles, untying the leather laces of their steel-toed
safety boots, and giving up their rage in the long, slow flush
of warmth and pressure swooshing up my body from heel to head.
Then there was an internal collapsing. A long-deactivated part
of me unwound helplessly and manifested as a full-size tantric sob
inhabiting my body. Calmly, the girl gathered up my feet. Undaunted
by their ugliness, she held them tenderly as nursing infants,
lifted them to her breasts, massaging and caressing
while she looked them over. After awhile, she was somewhat less
gentle: perhaps she held them then as the sous chef charged
with murdering the baby quail hardens himself for the task ahead.
She gasped a little, horrified, I imagined, by the thick rinds of calluses,
the cracked and blackened nails, the custard-colored orbs of dead skin
she would have to overcome. I think I even heard her moan—alarmed
by the extensive renovation that lay ahead, or anguished at my sacrifice:
my desecration of the gift of soft and polished feminine feet.

Behind my closed eyes, my mother was up off her knees,
and moving back in time, becoming younger. Now
she was tottering and mincing along in cheap, post-war stilettos
on her way to labor in the typing pool. At the end of a long day,
her feet cramped and pulsing, she'd pry them off, and drop them
with a groan. *My poor old dogs,* she'd moan, her Liverpudlian tones
just right for the image she'd composed. Now, *my* old dogs
were guiltily reborn as a pair of pampered lap dogs in a pedicurist's palms.

The soul moves when the soul moves, the Ancients all admonished.
Just so, enlightenment comes as it will, when it will, as unembarrassed
by squalor as unmoved by glamour. Thus, when my battered feet
were plunged inside a bowl of melted paraffin, and left

to bubble there deliciously, something ratcheted into place.
The moment shaped itself into a needle, and there I hung:
impaled on the epiphany. A massive ur-sound, subterranean
and private as a fart, emerged unbidden from my throat . . .

All this corporeality keeps conjuring my mother. She's back,
cuddled in the center curve of the 1950s gold-flecked sofa
beside my father. Her nylon-stockinged feet are in his lap.
He's turning up his cuffs. A well-known rule is that my father
is the only one allowed to touch my mother's feet. We don't
know why. I see him starting to massage them both,
uncrimping her toes, and threading his fingers in between
to excavate the sweaty, fragrant nits of hidden grime.
Now, he is kneading her swollen soles until she groans
and leans back, closing her eyes, as relaxed and somehow *open*
as if she's lying there alone. Eventually, the faintly damp
and private odor of my mother's tired feet is released into the air.

And that is where I am—mentally stranded in a perverse version
of the primal scene, starring my father's hands on my mother's feet,
my own feet stunned by an underwater orgasm in the foot bath's
gurgling whirlpool—when a voice plucks me from my pleasures.
"You want razor?" my pedicurist asks. She's holding up the rasp,
displaying above a clean white towel, the two-sided shaver
with which she will trim corns and prune back calluses
in her search for the beauty I've abandoned.
Yes! I say to her. *I want the razor!* Use it to remove
all that separates me from the simple pleasures.
Shave off the rage of the workers, the fear of the victims,
the shame of the survivors. Prune back my lost eros,
and train it to survive in a small container, confined
and stunted as a bonsai tree. Mow down the scourge
of oedipal envy that still carries a bite. Wrap it up
in a white towel and take it away with the gray-tinged nits
of curling skin shaved from the calluses rimming my heels,

and just let me lie here blissfully for awhile, enjoying
my first pedicure, transported back to those glorious moments
just after birth, half a century ago, when my mother
must have held me close all morning long, marveling
at my brand new beauty, inventorying my fingers, counting
my toes, and clasping tight in both her hands the twin
unspoiled beauties of my two perfect feet.

SHAMPOO GIRL

The war was on. Linda Oglethorpe's stepbrother had died
there—wherever it was—and she, our school's one and only
hippie, had sat through three periods weeping behind her silky
swath of ironed hair until someone drove her home to cry.
In Washington, Abbie Hoffman levitated the Pentagon
and Allen Ginsberg, on the other coast, read a poem
in full lotus position, naked. A man walked on the moon
and said something memorable. At Woodstock, teens
made love in mud. But all of this was pretty abstract
to me, hardly more than magazine covers or a quick story
on the black and white while I ate my dinner on a TV tray
and then rushed back to the privacy of my bedroom
to scrutinize emergent acne or calculate how to get so-and-so
to invite me to the junior prom . . . Otherwise,
how could I have spent each Saturday of 1968 and '69
in Wingo's House of Beauty untangling the back-combed
over-teased heads of lower middle class housewives
who hadn't been informed of women's liberation and still tortured
their hair into pageboys and bubble 'dos with wire rollers
and hair spray? And then came, each Saturday,
to submit themselves to me, conversing grimly
about husbands and varicose veins while, gently,
I combed them out and then lowered their heads,
large and heavy as spoiled cabbages,
into green ceramic basins. I fastened warm white towels
around their shoulders and tested the water on my wrist
as if bathing an infant. And then dispersed the shampoo's
fragrant mucus into their hair, directed hot needles of water
towards their scalps, drenched them, and scrubbed. They purred like cats
beneath my hands. I liked it there—the sharp fragrances
of peroxide and nail polish, the dull whine of the old-fashioned
chrome-hooded dryers. The way it took your mind off
everything troublesome and fastened it to a rat's nest
in a bleached blond pageboy, or a crochet hook used
to fish up strands of auburn hair through a punctured rubber cap
that covered a head being prepped for streaking.

If I'd really understood what was happening in the world
I couldn't have gone on, could I? Week after week, year after year,
cocooned in that place, washing heads for $1.50 an hour,
oblivious to napalm-covered little girls and whole villages
wiped out by nineteen-year-old American boys in helicopters
my parents paid taxes to reproduce as soon as they had crashed and burned.
I don't know what it means now, that I wasted my time that way
helping someone acquire the hairstyle she wanted,
as if nothing was more important than vanquishing
split ends and instructing someone in the fine art
of wrapping toilet paper, turban style,
around her head and spraying heavily, to keep it all
in place a week. Now I wonder how it was possible
to walk out at the end of the day, feeling as if
something worthwhile had been done, and to observe
the sun drown in the smoke-stained sky
and experience no sense of interconnectedness
and not think of burning villages and shattered countries,
while the war raged, the president lied, and 55,000 lay down
beneath the black wall and never rose to chastise me.

THE POLACK

The planes carrying us stateside after our tour had to ascend at a
really steep angle to avoid anti-aircraft fire from the North
Vietnamese. So, leaving, like everything else there, was really tense.
When we took off, it was overcast. But then we broke through
35,000 feet and the cloud cover at the same time. The sun stabbed
us through the windows it was so bright. Then the pilot came on the
P.A. and said, "Welcome home, gentlemen." And he put in a tape—
Richie Havens singing, "Here Comes the Sun," and everyone—I
mean everyone—was crying.
—A VETERAN OF THE VIETNAM WAR

He almost had to growl to say his own name,
Greggie Grzinsky, "that Polack kid from Buffalo,"
a big boy, always fighting, growing into the shape
of his father's despisal—*the best part of you, kid,
ran down my leg*—and hulking down, ashamed
inside his own body as if something essential
had been carved out of him and carried away,
and was moldering now, undiscovered,
in the decomposing garbage at the junkyard
or the dump. So when he went to war, it wasn't
really all that different, and he discovered himself
a superb soldier, a battalion commander who kept
a clear head and never lost a man, and killed, he supposed,
dozens, even hundreds, of the enemy, foreign people
he never saw and couldn't care about, blowing them up
from ten miles back. Still, war was war,
and even a hard man, even a growling dog of a man
with no soft center, found himself counting
the days until he was sprung from that humid
garden where fields were shallow pools of fecund
water alive with delicate sprouts of rice and buried
hand grenades. Where the sky could be a canopy
of tendriling trees or fragile ringlets of tropical flowers,
but other times exploded into psychedelic blossoms
of missile fire and ate itself up. The darkness and the feminine

odor of the lowering heat forced him to ponder his lost
best part, his father's ancient pleasure in the dark,
and how he must have turned away, sticky and separate,
after the act. Around him, the jungle steamed fragrantly, indifferent
as a whore rising to bathe in the Quonset brothel outside Da Nang.
So when the plane carrying him home at last
banked sharply in the sky, roaring, it seemed, almost
straight up, he suddenly jettisoned his father's life—
the immigrant child in Buffalo, New York, stumbling
over the syllables of his own name in a new language,
sponging his jacket of the rotten oranges and balls of mud
flung at his back as he walked to school, stopping his ears
to the incessant cawing of the wiry little Poles
fortunate enough to be born in America—*dirty Polack,*
stinking Polack—the two room tenement thick
with the smells of boiling cabbage and stuffed pirogi,
his mother's babushka, her blood-cracked hands
and terrified tongue. And then there was his father
all grown up at the center of a new life, a belt
in his hand, his shirt stained with beef blood
where he'd wiped the cleaver dawn to dusk,
the old syllables cracking cleanly in his mouth.
And there he was, too, laboring on into the night
hunched above the body of the boy's own mother,
and pulling out, the son realized now, to confound
conception, and rolling off and over in the dark
just a few feet distant from the body of his boy, curled
like a dog on a folded blanket spread thinly on the floor.
And then resting on his back, his dark grunt of satisfaction
filling the room with a kind of cloud, his hands
cupped on his groin to form a little sacramental space
devoted to the only place in life that gave him any pleasure.

And so, all those years later, to remember those words—
the best part—as the plane surges through the atmosphere

carrying him, finally, away from war, he sees himself
alive at last, a swimmer in a clear tear of human hope,
a globule of desire rising from the old life at the same time
that it falls, disconnecting from the site of his entire history
and burning in its tracks both painfulness and pleasure.

PEEP SHOW

We are coming down from our pedestal and up from the laundry room.
—BELLA ABZUG

When I want to, I can still wrench the years back to 1978,
and visit myself standing outside the Times Square
peep show. I'm wearing that hip-length, bias-cut,
gray tweed overcoat I used to love. It's swirling
in a flare above my straight-leg jeans and lace-up,
flat-heeled boots that were all the rage that fall.
There's still a decade to go before the mayor
will clear the streets of cheap sex and poverty.
So I'm standing on pavement clotted with dried-up discs
of hawked-out phlegm and chewing gum, and the air
is redolent with the odor of pot and filthy, unwashed
hair, and curbed pools of human waste glistening
in the gutter. Behind me, blacked out windows crawl
with crudely painted purple script. Some untutored
hand has filled the pane's dark glass with wormlike curlicues:
LIVE! NUDE! GIRLS! the window screams, are inside, dancing . . .

I must have forced my mind to curve itself acceptingly
around the fact of living girls dancing nude a few feet past
those painted windows I leaned upon. But what about their *price*?
Surely, the calm, dispassionate expression on my face belies
the shocking fact that a forty-second, glassed-in glimpse
of a young girl's mindless grinding in the bony basket
of her adolescent hips cost nothing but a quarter. *Not a penny more
than that.* A grimy satin g-string has unraveled from the fraying
of her fingers where she's shoved aside, again and again,
all shift long, the triangular remains of her violated privacy.
A plastic speaker rattles out the Rolling Stones. Woozily,
she strains and totters on platform heels to keep the beat.
Inside, the brand-new husband of my youth stands
before a metal slot, feeding quarters from the hoarded stash
I've saved for laundry till the window drops,
and the girl's revealed. He leans towards the mike's

black mouth and states his wish, standing there alone
in the small tight space of sticky musk and wadded Kleenex,
piling snow-like in the corners, as he'll tell me later.

I said: he was *standing there alone in the small tight space* . . .
But really, wasn't I there, too, a kind of same-sex
ghost pimp of that dancing, drugged-up girl incarcerated
in her slimy, sexless spot? For without my husband, without
my quarters, without desire redirected from my bridal
bed, the scene would not exist. But there it is, as indelible
as the opening chapter in a long novel where we look
to find the early life events that explicate the later complications
of the story's central plot. Thumbing back through the murky
chapters of the distant past, my text perplexes. I wonder *now*
what I was thinking *then*? I, who called myself a feminist,
and demonstrated for women's lib and civil rights.
What would my heroines have thought if they'd seen me
leaning there against the painted sign advertising the girls
for sale inside, my in-laws' ancient diamond solitaire weighting down
my clean left hand, sparkling in a brand-new setting?

                Now, it's like another life I lived
back then. Another planet. Times Square's urgent commerce,
its quick thrills and cheap bodies of bought sex are all gone.
As are the early months of failed marriage, and the craving lustful
appetites of youth. As are the mysteries of sex, and the hardy,
virile bodies of the years of procreation. Now the past unrolls
like fragile scrolls of text, almost illegible with overlapping lines
of script. I can't make out the words that might remind me
who that woman was, or what, leaning there, she might have thought.
Married just a month, was she perhaps uncertain
what the bonds of matrimony in that brand new age required?
and so she stood there on the sidewalk waiting for the man inside
as if he were a prince, as if he were her One True Love
from an earlier era she'd read about when she was young.
Like the heroines of those ancient stories, she just stood there,

stolid as an object. And now she is stuck there *in perpetuity.*
That girl who looks like I once looked. She goes on standing
on the filthy sidewalk as if she were anywhere but where she is:
waiting and waiting for something that was promised,
but now (she starts to realize) will never come.

HOMAGE TO CALVIN SPOTSWOOD

> Yet not for those,
> Nor what the potent victor in his rage
> Can else inflict, do I repent or change,
> Though changed in outward luster . . .
> —*Paradise Lost,* BOOK I

Because I couldn't bear to go back to the south side
of Richmond and the life I had led there—the blaring
televisions, the chained-up hounds, the cigarettes hissing
in ceramic saucers, the *not never's, I'm fixin' to's,*
the *ain'ts*—because anything at all was better than that,
I took the job. The four bucks an hour, the zip-front,
teal-colored, polyester uniform, the hairnets and latex gloves,
the intimate odors of piss and sweat, the eight hour
shifts of vomitus and shit, of death and death. And death . . .
Each day, I pinned on the badge that admitted me
to hell: nurse's aide on an oncology ward for terminal patients.

Calvin Spotswood was my first patient. His metal chart
proclaimed him: "Nonambulatory, terminal C.A." A Goner,
the docs called him, a noncompliant asshole they wheeled
like a dying plant, out of the sun, out of the way,
so he could wither and perish at his own speed, distanced
from those with a happier prognosis. Parked in a dim back room,
he went unheard when pain peeled him down to his disappearing center.

Calvin had dropped down through a chute in the day to day,
and skidded in for a landing on the flaming shores
of Stage III colorectal cancer. Nightly, he cooked there,
flipping back and forth on the grainy, Cloroxed sheets
like a grilling fish. Timidly at first, I bathed the hot grate
of his ribs with tepid water, the cloth I dipped
almost sizzling dry on his heaving chest. I hated the feel
of his skin, the intimacy of my hands on his body. I hated
the smell beneath his sheets, the odor of his mouth. I hated
to touch him—a dying man, a devil, trapped, alive, in hell.

                                    I feel
uncomfortable now, because he was black, imagining
Calvin as Milton's Satan, as if I am demonizing him unfairly,
or engaging in a stereotype based on race. But I had read the poem
and I recognized immediately the one who was "hurled headlong flaming"
from the gates of heaven, and "chained" for infinity "on the burning lake"
of his hospital bed. Like Lucifer, Calvin was a troublingly complex
anti-hero —a horrible person in many ways, stubbornly stupid,
had abused his nurses and cursed the doctors, refusing
the surgery that might have prolonged—or saved—his life.
He wouldn't be *unmanned,* he said, *shitting in a bag. No f-ing way.*
He said "f-ing," instead of the full blown word,
a kind of delicacy I found peculiar, and then endearing.
And though the tumor, inexorably, day by day, shut him down,
he wouldn't pray, or console himself in any of the usual ways. Each afternoon,
he turned away from the Pentecostal preacher who stood with his Bible
at the foot of his bed, and said his name kindly and asked to say
a prayer or lay his hands upon the burning body. *No f-ing way.*

The tumor grew until it bound itself into his stomach wall.
Each move he made extracted a fiery arrow of flaming pain
from his rotten gut. And when the house staff figured
they had him beat, and organized a betting pool on how soon old Calvin
would entrust himself to the surgeon's knife so he could eat
again, he still declined, still whined for pussy, porno mags,
and chicken fried in bacon grease. A third-year resident,
Harvard MD, wrote an order for the supper Calvin thought
he craved: mashed potatoes and buttered bread, a chicken-battered,
deep-fried steak. Beaming, our man consumed it while his doctor lingered
outside his door to await the inevitable result of the natural process
of human digestion . . . Here is where I need to remind you that this
was back when the old U.Va. hospital still stood, on the brick-curbed rim
of Hospital Drive, where the sign saying *Private* really meant white, a reminder
of what passed for health care in the segregated South.
Nurses still wore bobby-pinned, absurd white hats that looked
as if they were about to levitate off of their heads.

The RNs were white, the practicals, black.
And none of the docs, of course, were black.
But Calvin was, and the Civil Rights Act was a decade old,
so it was the New South, instead of the Old, where Calvin consumed
his last good meal, deluded into thinking a black man in the South
had finally won. An hour later, he knew he'd lost, and patients
two floors down could hear him screaming from the mouth
of the flaming crater he filled with curses.

Night after night, wrist deep in the tepid water I bathed him with,
I stood at his beside and tried to change him from hot to cool
and listened to him discourse maniacally on the mysteries of gender:
born again, he'd be a woman in slick red panties, a streetwalking
whore in high-heeled sandals and torn, black hose, opening his legs
for paper money, filling his purse with bucks to spend.
How anyone was granted a life like that he could never comprehend:
getting paid to fuck. His greatest treasure had been a dark red Pontiac
he'd drive down D.C.'s 14th Street on the lookout for whores and games of cards.
He'd been a lumberjack, he revealed one night. A quelling job,
and measured with his hands sphered into a circle, the muscles
jettisoned to illness. His strength had been his pride.
Now, he was a wiry and diminutive, sick stick of a man,
shriveled by a tumor. The image of his former power resided
in the two huge wives who guarded his door, one white, one black.
Passing between the corporeal portals of their womanly flesh,
my pale-toned puniness frightened me. But even in the final stages
of a violently invasive terminal carcinoma, nothing daunted Calvin—
not even the quarter ton of dominating, loud-mouthed women
with whom he had conceived six children. I marveled
at the unrancorous way they held each other, their cheap clothing
crinkling noisily, releasing that funky odor big people carry.
Their decaled fingernails, their huge, flopping breasts, their ornate hairdos—
the one teased up and lacquered high in place, the other cornrowed
flat with beads—their flamboyance so obvious I couldn't help
but apprehend what Calvin Spotswood thought was hot in women.
Not me, of course, skinny college girl with straight brown hair,

and wire-rimmed glasses, dog-earing Book I of *Paradise Lost . . .*
What Calvin adored were the superfluous extras I tried to delete—
fat and loudness, clandestine odors of secreted musk.

At the end, cupping his withered, hairless testicles
in my cool, white palm because he asked me to, it wasn't anything
like witnessing a death. More like the birth of a new world, really,
he was entering alone. The little universe of sperm that twirled
beneath my hand, he was taking with him. On the burning bed,
his mouth lolled open in forgotten, wasted pleasure,
and I saw in my mind images of the South's strange fruit, the old photos
bound into books of black men who'd transgressed, swinging
heavily from trees. But Calvin was uncatalogued among
their demeaned postures and living deaths. His name was written
in the *dramatis personae* of a slimmer text, an epic poem about the fall
from grace of a defiant, finger-flipping Beelzebub who dared
to challenge the creator of a world where black men swung
from the limbs of trees for admiring the backside of fair-skinned girls.
Calvin was the one kicking holes in the floor of that so-called heaven to hasten
his eviction. And so I touched him. I did, and stroked him even closer
to the edge, marveling at the force of ravaged life, at the inscrutable
nature of a God who would keep alive a man who claimed to *hate his f-ing guts*
and nail into my mind forever, Calvin Spotswood in his final hours,
undiminished, unredeemed, unrepentant, his poor black body burning and burning.

CROWNS

for Philip Levine

Around the time I first read the poetry of Philip Levine,
my teeth were fixed. Two or three hundred bucks
(I've forgotten now) purchased a brand new me,
two porcelain crowns. In the dentist's chair, my midget
canines were filed down to sharp, bright points
hardly larger than the bronzed end of a Bic
pen, then crammed in the black-backed caps
of two hardened, china fakes. No more
covering my mouth to obscure the evidence
of faulty genes. No more tears at images
embezzled from graduation picnics
when Darrell Dodson picked me up and slung me
in the pool, and someone took a picture
of my lips slacking back to reveal my gums
in what appeared to be a scream. No more breezes
winding through the gappy pickets of my ill-grown
teeth and down my throat. No more worrying
some boy would snag his tongue in the zigzagged bulkhead
of my upper row, and bring us both to blood.

I'll love Levine forever for confessing his own struggles
with orthodontia, his rot-plagued "Depression mouth,"
a dentist called it, his cavities and root canals, his occipital pain,
for his photograph in *Antaeus,* the summer of '78,
the stained and crooked slabs parked compellingly
behind his grin. Our teeth connected us before the poetry,
he, from the immigrant onion-eaters and temperate tipplers
of Manischewitz. I, from a long line of tannin-stained
Irish Catholics who smoked themselves to fragile
states of calcium depletion, and a recent run of Carolina
gritballs, too poor to brush, too ignorant to care their teeth
retired in early middle age. I can see them now, perplexed
before an apple's crispy rind, frustrated by a succulent, stringy rack
of pork ribs barbequed in the side lot of Earlene Worsham's

service station south of town. Levine would have understood my uncles,
enthroned on plastic-covered kitchen chairs patched with tape,
their work boots kicking up mucky clouds of chiggery dirt,
their pick-ups parked nearby, shotguns in the rack,
sucking on cheap beers and harsh cigarettes,
their nails starved by nicotine to yellow curls, the car grease
embedded permanently in the creases of their hands.

When I met him, he was such a mensch, massive
in my mind, but in the flesh, something touching
about his shoulders in the worn tweed jacket, something
vulnerable in his feet in an ordinary pair of soiled, white sneakers.
He opened his mouth to laugh, one side rising up
like it does, in that derisive gesture that seems, at first, a sneer,
and I remembered my mother flexing back her lips to remove
delicately, with two stained fingers, just so, a fleck of tobacco
lodged between her teeth, and saw again my father flossing at the table
with the torn-off cover of a paper book of matches,
then stubbing out his butt in the yellowed, oily pod of broken yolk
that was hemorrhaging across his breakfast plate.

I can face those images now without the shame
I carried in the days before the poetry of Phil Levine
liberated me. I can look at anything now, because I keep
his picture in my mind and his poems in my pocket.
I can stand my life because I wear the crown he constructed
for people like me—grocery checkers, lube jobbers, truck drivers,
waitresses—all of us crowned with the junkyard diadems
of shattered windshields and rusty chains, old pots
with spit tobacco congealing inside, torn screen doors
and gravestones in the front yard, just five short steps from life to death . . .

So there is my family with their broken beer bottles
and patched shoes, their mutts chained in a back yard
carved from a stingy pine woods, on cheap land
out near the county dump where the air swells with the perfume

of trash, a circle of them playing poker in a trailer somewhere
in the woods, or razoring the state decal from the windshield
of a ransacked wreck to transfer to my brother's car.
Or cleaning fish on the back porch and throwing the guts
to the tick-clogged dogs, or frying venison in a cast-iron pan
and stinking up the house with that heavy smell, showing
the buck's big balls in a plastic canister that once held salt.
Or burning tires in a field some autumn, scumming
the sky with a smoky, cursive black they can't even read
but inhale poisonously again and again.

And there I am, walking along tolerantly now, with Phil Levine,
his poems in my pocket, his good rage gathered in my heart
and I can love them again, the way I did in the years before
I saw what they were and how the world would use them
and accepted the fact they were incapable of change.
We're in a field I used to love, a redbone coonhound running ahead
her ears dragging the edges of the goldenrod till they are tipped
in pollen, like twin paintbrushes dipped in gilt. And the world
is hunting dogs and country music and unschooled voices
bending vowels and modest kitchen gardens where late tomatoes
are tied up with brownish streamers of old nylon hose.
The vast way your chest expands when the sun gradually sets
in mid-fall in central Virginia. The tobacco barns glimmering
in last light, the chinks darkening now, the slats solidifying at the close of day
and your mind opening up like the pine forest swishing fragrantly overhead
way up in the dark that is coming, but remains, for the moment,
beautifully at bay.

DOGTOWN, 1957

In the piney, pink stria of summer morning skies, we awoke
to the muted, moan-like howling of the hungry redbones
locked in their chain-link compounds. They lived their lives
like that: locked in wire cages until released to hunt, fragmented
images of earlier expeditions flickering in and out of whatever
consciousness they possessed, exciting them to live. Maybe
somewhere in their genetic memories there existed remnant
images of the fleeing slaves their ancestors had pursued north
through the boggy bottoms of the Dismal Swamp to Dogtown,
where freed slaves and poor whites had subsisted for a century,
economically bonded in perpetuity to the gentrified bastards
living north of the river, who valued nothing more than saving
the fabled cobblestones of Monument Avenue from urban renewal.
There, on that broad swath of grassy boulevard, the horsebacked
Confederate generals, deceased in war, cantered statically
through eternity, unaware their dream was dead.

And here in Dogtown, across the river from that genteel boulevard
with its antique mansions and art museums, with its tennis courts
and flower gardens, we didn't seem to be going anywhere either.
We arose each day and heard the members of our family
clambering past each other for access to the solitary bath
that lacked a tub, our unkempt toenails clicking on the scarred wood floors.
No one spoke, but we could hear the thwonging hiss of my father's
early morning piss throughout that house, and the foamy scratch
of my uncle's razor on his chin as he shaved around his cigarette.
Already, the day's allotment of acrid smoke and malodorous saucers
of stubbed-out butts had begun to mount. The smell stuck in our hair,
in our clothes, turning them rancid. Someone switched on an AM radio.
Someone stirred brown-black granules of instant coffee in a cup of boiling water.
Then, among the ashtrays and the matchbooks on the table top,
we poured out bowls of cold cereal from paper boxes, and fell into them,
lapping the milk like famished creatures. Outside, the other

creatures shook the fencing of their pens, hurling themselves
full-length on the chain link walls while we screamed at them
to hush. But they were dogs, and knew no better. Undeterred
by our demand for silence, they went on howling, mindlessly, inside their cages.

CIGARETTES AND MATCHES

It's my first memory really, earlier even
than standing on the stoop of my parents' apartment,
arms extended toward the great green globe of ball
my grandmother is tossing toward me, her sweet
smile crooked in her face, her eyes filled with shy love.
Earlier even than that prelapsarian moment—the birth
of love, my grandmother beautiful as Venus floating
on Botticelli's shell—is being sent to fetch the cigarettes
with the matches that were always wedged beneath
the cellophane wrapper of the neat, red pack.
Paul Mawls, my mother, British, called them.
Pell mell, my father said, more brutally American, more
accurate inadvertently, rushing to stuff one in his mouth
upon awakening, after love, during meals.

In the winter version of this memory, I see myself
in the cold front room of the little house on Royal Avenue,
the damp, chill air staticizing the objects in the room
as if to confer some meaning I can understand.
I see myself as if among the furnishings of a lesser known
but tragic myth—the cigarettes and matches, instruments
of death, laid out on a table next to her side of the tumbled
blankets, on the windowsill, next to his. Flanking the bed,
ceramic saucers filled with ashes, their harsh fragrance
dulled by the unheated air, as solemn as the twin urns
on either side of a medieval donor's portrait. Dislodging them
from their interpretative settings, I'd bring them back
among the light and warmth of my aunt and uncles, my parents,
until I failed to comprehend them as objects again,
and they became nothing more than white tubes
of fragrant, flaming pleasure desired by adults.
I carried them in a gingerly fashion, finger and thumb
pinched together so I was barely touching, or wrapped them
in the clean white sleeve of a tissue or a paper towel. Even then,
I must have understood their killing power, the lust my parents
had conceived for them. The little scrapes of sulfur

on sand paper, the sudden flare, the drawing in,
the sucked-in cheeks and squinting eyes tearfully assaulted
by tobacco smoke—that was the scenario that drove me out,
that took them—pell mell—away from me sitting in the back seat
of the car on the way to church. They became mere shapes
of parents—heads buzzing, bodies jazzed, floating off somewhere
distant, alone and together.

In the summer, after dinner, running in the backyard
with a cleaned-out mayonnaise jar, holes punched in the lid,
a firefly house, out of my body for a moment, I'd still be
ordered in to fetch the smokes, the cigarettes
and matches laying on the kitchen table beside the plates,
butts stubbed out in the dregs of supper, fried hamburger and onions,
collards and creamed potatoes, where someone
always smoked before the meal was done. Carrying them back
to my parents sitting on the wood porch steps in the humid dark,
I came to fear the little orgy of pleasure that excluded me—
the brief flare of orange flame, and then the steady, tiny glow
of red ash sparkling, heads tilted close so he could pass his, lit,
to hers and share a match. The way their bodies seemed to drain,
almost instantly, of tension . . . Even in the dark, I could see them
and they were just like the fireflies trapped in my glass jar
with a spear of grass, unaware of any imminent demise,
still sparkling in their beauty, like stars contained in a god-sized fist
as if some titan had plucked a few comets from the firmament
for his toddler's pleasure and shook them up in a giant's jar
to watch them glow, beauteously, for a few moments and then
unconcernedly dropped them in the grass when other pleasures
beckoned, and left them there, slowly, to perish.

OLD PAIN

Now that my father is dead, the mere sight
of cigarettes and matches makes me ill,
and the smell of ashy death in a chronic smoker's
mouth recalls his painful final years, the yellowed
claws his fingers twisted to, the clanking tanks
of bottled air, the heaving slab of slack flesh
his chest sustained. . . . Sometimes, even now,
unaware, I inhale a fragrant waft of tobacco
emanating from some gangly stranger in a cheap suit
hurrying past on the streets of a Southern city,
and I am lifted from the stupor of the everyday.
My heart rises in a ripe bubble of joy, calling up
the memory of my young father and our early years
together when it still seemed possible he might learn
to cherish his only daughter. Tears rinse my eyes
with sudden, unexpected heat and I have to
pull myself over to the side of the walk
and hide in the shadow of a tall building.
As if I were the driver of a car who has barely
avoided a catastrophic wreck, I stand there awhile
and calm myself. The way a smoker, perhaps,
might need to take a break when things get shaky,
and the urge grows for some chemical adjustment
that will hijack him back to his favorite place,
where he's almost untouchable, and just barely visible
in the smoke-filled space between him and the rest of us.

THE DIVORCE

All that failed was imagination. Hers,
that clung without remorse or pity
to vicious words and bruised shoulders,
to a kick down the steps, and the shattered
louvers of a wooden door gashed
by an airborne wrench. Or the car
in the vector of its slippery skid.
On the rainy road, that afternoon
in winter, a Sunday so long ago. Yes,
it was the car, she finally decided,
more than anything else: stalled
and tilted in the muddy ditch.
The gear shift was still in third,
and the rear view reflected him stomping
away, angry all over, hysterical even
in his thinning hair. She was sure
he was betting she'd fetch him as she had
in the past, bleating in terror, pleading, *stay.*

A brief series of dull-toned beeps
announced the key was still lodged
in the ignition. The radio purred, the heat
whispered, the wipers wiped. Almost everything
went on as before. Swiping clear
a temporary arc to peer beneath,
the wipers revealed the empty road
that led to town, the steel-fenced
pastures on either side, the animals miserable
in icy rain. Looking backwards through the mirror,
she felt weather thickening the distance
between them. She couldn't imagine anything
ever it was possible to change. There was his same old
overcoat, the cheap cloth shoes. And there, too,
was she, the same as ever, weak and afraid,

seat-belted in a car her beloved had tried
to wreck. God, she was weary. How simple
really, to slide at last, into the driver's seat,
to turn the key and roar away—
up and out of the ditch forever.

BEANS ON TOAST

Fondling the plump pads of midlife fat at my waist
and thighs, I think of pork and beans on buttered toast,
that make-do meal of early life. The 12th or 13th day
of the two-week cycle of my parents' paltry pay would find
the kitchen denuded of all beef and cheese, potatoes
consumed, bread eaten down to stubbed, stale ends.
Then we'd burrow in the cabinets for surplus tins
of canned red beans purchased from the supermarket's
half-priced bin of dents and dings. Perhaps, we would have
borne it better if we'd recalled the noble nature of nasty haggis,
another meal derived from dregs my Celtic mother's kin
prepared in times long past—the boiled protuberant
stomach of a sheep stuffed with heart- and liver-studded porridge,
then oven-boiled for hours till it swelled with seasoned, gaseous pressure
and threatened to explode. Haggis, in a way, bejeweled the common person's
gut, defied its origin in the undesired cuts the butcher would just as soon
throw out. Haggis was a celebration of the trials of life
in peat-stained, low-roofed one-room cottages where quarrelsome
families of twelve or more, ruled by genetically-encoded impulsivity,
subsisted meagerly for generations. To pipe in—with prayers and toasts
to Robbie Burns—the haggis on a bed of spud was a conquest of sorts.

Perhaps if we had thought to serve our meager, almost-payday meal
on our one and only silver-plated tray, we might have seen
our lives in some kind of new relief, and bent our heads
to our beans on toast with a kind of pride, uplifted by the way
our mother folded paper napkins beside our plastic plates,
and allowed ourselves to forget her angry little hands
stained with freckles cranking open the tin of beans
and picking out the tiny bits of soaked white fat
and throwing them down into the paper bags
of kitchen garbage bulging at her feet.
And convinced ourselves to forget our father ignoring
our poverty behind the veil of his newspaper and the brown glass walls

of his bottles of beer. Perhaps we might have come to love
the way we bowed our heads and used the manners
we'd been taught, even as we went on sinking and sliding,
sliding and sinking.

When I Was the Muse

When the painter said, *OK, you guys,*
take off your clothes! I startled at the plural,
assuming I'd been engaged to model by myself.
But then the dark-skinned god I knew as Aaron
from my econ class unzipped his jeans,
and dropped them, grinning, on the floor.
So I did, too, and clambered up beside him
on the plywood box that elevated us above
the clutch of paint-stained easels. Thoughtfully,
the students posed our naked bodies. Someone fluffed
the crispy hair between my legs into a dark brown
bristling fan. And someone pinched the sides
of Aaron's face to pinken up his cheeks.
Privately, I installed myself inside that mental space
where I had hidden as a child when the world
could be aborted no other way . . .

It was part of my plan to walk unclothed
among the portraits my unclad body
had provoked. So when we broke
for lunch, the students lunging in a herd
out back to smoke, I sallied forth. If you had asked me
then why I modeled, I'd have said,
to overcome my bourgeois insecurities,
to combat my fear of what might happen
if I showed myself completely naked
to someone else. But if you asked me now?
I'd describe the experience of walking among
a museum of strangers' images devoted to oneself,
and tell you what a privilege it was to see myself
the varied ways that others did.

Some silly fellow had painted nipples on me the size
and shape of frying eggs. Another jokester
had shrunk them down as small as M&M's.
But someone serious and sad had shared a vision

of my head as a clotted orb of hair and mouth,
and brushed in underneath, a body headless
as the horseman in the myth. Then I seemed
to walk into the darkroom of my mind's own eye
and saw the disconnected self I'd always felt inside
but never known: a complicated, unsmiling creature
with a fear-tinged face. Around her the aura of something
golden was fighting with whip-like straps of something black.
She was staring straight into the future, trying
to get out, and to conceal her fear, completely unaware
of how it glistened and glowed, and how irresistible
it had been for the artist to spread it across the canvas
so that everyone could see.

THE HATCHING

Burning in our twin scarlet fevers,
we were laid out, feet to feet,
on the worn, gold sofa, my brother and me.
A doctor stood above us, his forehead
pleated into folds of mottled flesh.
Our young mother stood in her winter coat
smoking the butt of a cigarette in the cold
dank air of our home. Behind her, unheated
rooms flared with unmade beds and stale twists
of soiled laundry. If perhaps she sought a brief
oblivion in nicotine, I should not blame her now.
For the furnace was shot, and no odors of dinner
cooking wafted from the kitchen, and our father
was not there. We saw him in our mind's eye
several miles away, leaning on the bar, seeking
his own relief in a cheap bottle of bitter beer.

To make us well, the doctor plunged his needles
in our naked rumps, and pulled the blankets tight
beneath our chins. And then—for reasons I cannot
conceive, and so I call it grace—removed from his car's
dark trunk, thick platters of old music encased
in paper sleeves. He carried them inside where we lay, burning.
On our ancient player: *The Nutcracker Suite,*
some strange and delicate food afloat in the air I swallowed
hungrily with my ears.
                                    And when I turned
from the harsh click of the needle's arm resettling
itself in its metal saddle, the world was stained glass,
my body a delicate canvas of skin over bone.
Something had once been painted there beautifully
and with care. And if it had worn away over the years,
or grown encased in a kind of shell? I suddenly saw
I could get back my beauty. I could peck my way out
like any young god, or a duckling, the black swan

hatching in a nest of white, the dark hum
of music in a small, tight place that resists
giving way till the final moment. Then it shudders
apart in an orgy of exit, and the shell—*the shell cracks open.*

2

LOUISIANA, LATE SUMMER

Because our bodies have been claimed
by humidity, we walk around in our heads
in the heat, squatting in the backroom
to paint a baseboard, sweat
pouring down in fragrant runs,
the ghosts of different body parts
asserting themselves with distinctive odors.

Overhead, a fan twirls lackadaisically,
collecting spores. Far back in the closet,
a light mold, transported here by some
primeval wind, festers on the toe
of a suede shoe. It pours its cheap
mold life into ignominy and plans
the destruction of the entire world.

SHEET: A Psychology

for William Christenberry

Some people have told me that this subject is
not the proper concern of an artist or of art. On
the contrary, I hold the position that there are
times when an artist must examine and reveal
such strange and secret brutality. It's my expres-
sion and I stand by it.
     —W. C.

I.
Because that form
Is still powerful to me

I went into the landscape
Never did I dream

a wedge of white wings
rising into the herald
of a hunter's twenty-two
and falling, marked

If I could take that
Form—the pyramidal
Hooded head—and transpose
This feeling that I possess
About memory . . . Beautiful
The way it cracked

into a bed of snow
destroyed by blood

II.
It was dark
And the street lights
Were on

Ed said, I'm Jewish
I'm not going inside

Old marble steps
To the second floor

Eyes glaring
Through the eyehole slits

I went out of the building
Just like that
The form entered me

A death of blizzard.
A murder of white.

How could I
As a human being
Let it go by?

III.
more than a few held the heft
of pain in their own
hands and judged the weight
too much to bear

and so drove it
down the road
to the homes of people
different from themselves
who wore no sheets
and walked about naked
in their pain

If you thought of the picture
As a dream or an apparition

but someone ignited it
and—through a plate glass
window—hurled a sheet of
pain wrapped around
a rock the size of a melon,
a cocktail of fire, a can
of gas. Whatever it was
it splattered on the baby's
bed and sprawled upright
in a flaming sheet
of gorgeous light.

IV.
These were tortured and/or
Bound & some had hot wax
Poured over them.

V.
Time goes by.
He hefted himself
into the cab of the pickup,
arranging the fabric in
folds, lifting it delicately
above his ankles.
He drove away
laughing, one hand,
on the wheel, the other
scrabbling in the melting
ice of the Styrofoam
cooler. *Nothing more*
Than a distant feeling. He wanted
one more beer. He opened
the window and hawked
a thin stream of blue-black

haw into the white dust
at the side of the road
and drove away from that ruined
image *that building on a back country
road with no windows and no doors*

VI.
*The places that still exist
Things that I grew up with
A memory house, a group of similar
Forms, covered in white wax
I can't explain why—stabbed,
And pinned and strapped up
To various and sundry things
The things I grew up with—what you see
Is what it is . . . An environment is
An environment—you have to
Walk into it—Black memory
Form, Memory form with Coffin,
Memory Form Dark Doorway,
I was always attracted to the warped
Shapes, the strange and secret brutality*
Right at the heart of it—*I've done
A lot of work there over the years . . .*

PHOTO BY WILLIAM CHRISTENBERRY

Akron, Alabama, ca. 1960

This is what it was like to grow up
down there, then. A pretty place
but desolate. The signs that are supposed
to tell you what to do, or be, or buy
are faded to the point of inarticulation.
You surmise people used to talk
about everything you need to know
but have grown silent for some reason.
A black man sat down in a soda shop
to eat a bite, and terrified, it seemed, the patrons.
I was there in that tense silence,
licking my strawberry cone, and it was
just like this picture of kudzu in winter,
the prettiness all covered over
with something growing too fast,
enshrouding the landscape with a sinewy
fabric that lives off the lives of others.
Or this next one of the house and car
in Akron, Alabama. The house is beat-up
and rusty, but habitable. You could live there
fine until something happens—a cross flaming
on the uncut lawn, or your house-girl's husband
with his foot shot off. That blue car's
been in the yard forever just waiting
for you to need it, and now you do.
So you head out, past the washer on the porch
and down the walk. You get in and realize
you're not going anywhere: it's up on blocks,
overrun by families of mice and birds. Why
did you never notice that before? How stuck here
you are with the blank sky and the fallen fences, the awful
unexplained silences of the South.

SQUARE EGG

When your email came with its depressing
message, I was having coffee. The dogs
were gnawing on biscuits in their beds,
and the low-pitched tone of the I-Mac the kids
had just abandoned let me know you were entering
my space. I clicked and opened, and there
you were: your email style as distinctive
as the smell of your mouth I still recall
after all these years. On the other side
of the kitchen wall, the washer rumbled
in the laundry room, and I felt a vibratory
swell ascend my legs and thighs in a watery rush
until it stopped, dead center, and nestled
in the archives of our privacy.

Reading your complaint about your lack of ties at 53,
untethered—*still*—to home or kin or pet, I recalled
a gift you bought me once: a silly, orange-tinted,
plastic cube, trademarked Square Egg Maker,
and how perverse it felt to press the still-warm
peeled-clean, hard-boiled egg inside, and close
the top, reshaping something elemental as an egg.

I called it Humpty for those few, brief weeks—
the little egg we turned, together, into a child. The one
you wouldn't *name* a child because I had to have it
scraped away. Legend claims that Humpty
kept his roundness and his hardness, for awhile.
But then he fell, and cracked himself to death. His yolk
poured out like mustard-colored blood. And when I lay
upon the table, and fit my heels in cold, steel slots,
allowing light to ply my darkest place, my yolk bled, too.

A Square Egg Maker might have saved our tiny egg
from Humpty's fate, and set it upright safely on the rim
of a breakfast plate, or the cool, curved lip of ceramic tile

on the kitchen counter where we loved to cook.
There, squared off and balanced on its bottom,
it might have throve, protected from the tumult
of our youthful passion. But it remained itself,
our little egg: unsquared and rounded, so elliptical and slick,
it could not resist the steep, declining edge of great, failed love.
And so it toppled, and just like Humpty in the fairy tale,
fell to gluey pieces in a pool of spewed-out albumen and ivory-
colored chips of shell, and the awful, ruined,
blood-streaked yolk.

LATE APOLOGY TO DORIS HASKINS

Come in, lone black girl, and sit among us.
And if there are twenty whites and only
one of you? No matter. New laws say
it must be so, and that we should
ignore the inequality that clouds
our visions of each other.
                              And so—
we sit here through the dragging day,
clock hands lagging maddeningly,
lessons sidelined, watching you
not watching us—your head
with its plethora of plastic barrettes,
your neat white socks creaming
your ankles. We circle you, sniffing.
And no one dares to enter the restroom
after you, perchance to occupy
the cool white seat you might have sat
upon for brief relief. And not one
of us will march beside you to the lunchroom
or the asphalt field where we play our games.
Each day, we hope the threats of bombs your presence
summons to what used to be our all-white school
will come again. For hours, then, we'll be out of class,
and free to wallow on the green front lawn, ignoring you
sitting off to the side, alone as usual, your plaid-skirted lap
filled with the torn-up blooms of buttercups.

We don't know why you are among us, or what
your presence means, or why we must attend
the mystery you make—a little girl who's more or less
identical to us despite the tales our parents tell.
Evenings, we watch them demonstrating on the TV news
in long, hot lines outside the board of education.
We read their signs and memorize the close-ups

of their faces twisted up with hate.
We watch them, as we eat our meals
on trays before the screen.

                              Your family
must watch them, too, before they kill the set
and send you off to bathe and pray and sleep.
Perhaps your mother stands, like mine,
late into the night, pressing flat the wrinkles
in your skirt with a hot iron, her mind
crowded with old terror she no longer
has the energy to fight. In the morning,
she will send her only daughter—a girl of ten—
forward into new light to vanquish it at last.
As will mine send forth *her* only daughter
to face the other side of your mother's terror.
And we will sit beside each other, Doris, gleaming
in our brand new classroom, sanctioned by the law,
spelling unfamiliar words, and calculating
complicated sums.

AT THE GYNECOLOGIST

I wouldn't wish this birthday on anyone in the world.
—DR. B., SEPTEMBER II, 2001

Around her in the waiting room,
basketballs of skin stretch tight
above the wriggling lumps
of bodies almost-born.

Menopausal now, *her* womb's
at rest, emptied of the eggs
that flowed out monthly
in a crimson show of forty years.

On a soundless screen, tiny
as an ultrasound, two towers
tumble down as easily
as children's blocks in chutes

of smoke and falling people.
Strangers' sons and daughters,
doused in diesel fuel avalanche
to the streets below.

Somehow, the frightful sight
recalls the way the body
of a full-grown infant presses
past the agonizing boundaries

of its mother, and how her hips
split open to receive
the crowning orbs
of boney skull, the slithery

bodies that gush out after,
the exultation of expulsion.
But no one here
wants to go forward

into *this* future. Hunching
tighter above their human cargoes,
new mothers cling, for now,
to what will be expelled

despite them. That empty space
onscreen—flames above disaster—
is where they'll land as stunned
and bloodied as the rest of us.

Cultural Diversity

Mr. Greenberg was her father's boss.

Carefully, her parents explained
how different he was from them.

How he didn't believe
in Jesus.

There was going to be
a barbeque for the office
staff in their back yard
and she had to be sure
not to serve Mr. Greenberg
any of the pork sausages
or spareribs because
he was a Jew.

(Someone who didn't
believe in Jesus, reiterated
her parents.)

All afternoon, she worked
the grill, carefully reserving
at all times three all-beef burgers
isolated, over on the side, above
the cooler coals
where she could quickly
reach them with her spatula
when Mr. Greenberg
approached with his gaping
open bun, his allotment of lettuce
and tomato, his mound of slaw,
and his appetite which seemed
no different from that of
everyone else who had accepted
Jesus Christ as their personal savior

and so earned the privilege of the garlicky
knockwurst she tended at the center
of the flame, pricking its sides
with a long fork so its tender juices
would drip onto the coals and tantalize
each of them equally with their spicy fragrance.

SHOTGUN FACE

Tell me—Emily Dickinson demanded—
                              How do people live without thoughts—
But how do people live without *faces* was the question
clamoring in the shattered mask of cyclopic, resewn flesh
beneath the long, blond hair of the boy we anointed
our local horror. Once, he'd been one of us—strolling
barefoot to class, sharing a joint. Now, on medical leave,
he patrolled the campus, belligerent and unapologetic,
encased within a shroud of stitched-together scars
he had learned to inhale through, and eat around,
and had *somehow* figured out how to live in spite of . . .

                              Because we couldn't look away,
we memorized his image—the missing eye, the absent
infrastructures of chin and jaw. Compulsively, we rehearsed
his act: what used to be his mouth—a twisted crescent
gash of open flesh, dripping like the entrance to a cave—
suggested he'd placed the weapon there, but then misfired.
Rocked back (we'd heard) in his father's recliner,
speakers blasting, he'd have been so high
(we theorized) he never even registered
the bone-rattling clack of the shotgun's muzzle
settling itself on his lower row of teeth. *Something*
went wrong, we kept repeating, parsing it out,
comparing our different readings. Resolute
to the end, or had he changed his mind,
but failed to abort after his toe, wedged
in the trigger, had already flexed?

                              Barely past childhood,
we knew almost nothing then, and spent our days
doing close readings of esoteric texts, irrelevant
to almost everyone on the planet. Thus, when we ferreted
down inside our undeveloped critical theories
and applied them in search of a plausible interpretation,

the proximity of a man who'd willingly destroyed
his very own face, and survived to ruin our world
with his horrifying image, wrenched out of orbit
our evolving philosophies . . .

                    Now I think we didn't really want
to know what he'd been thinking, or what he'd felt
at that moment we could not imagine anyone
but a literary character would ever reach. And *that's*
why we resented the brazen, unvictimized way
in which he occupied our field of vision. Enough of him
and his blaring image, his *real politik* . . . We wanted back
our text-based certainties about the structures of tragedy,
and to move through that world undisturbed by his man-sized
facsimile of self-destruction, our debate about his hands
with their long, guitar-picking nails, and how they must have
clattered noisily through the box of shells. How was it possible
they had failed to call him back with their promise of music?

                    So when he wheeled about
on the green lawns unfurling from the college grounds,
and positioned his monstrous remnant of a head so it was pointing
in our direction and strolled forward as if he were an ordinary
person, we couldn't take it. But all we could combat him with
were words: "Failed Suicide Walking," our lips pursing
around too many syllables, our tongues taking so much time
we couldn't help but disappear inside the structural dynamics
of how he got that way. When someone in a class on Latin
prosody blurted SHOTGUN FACE, we hunkered down
inside those three brief beats he called amphimacer.
They stalled us on the image and drove our minds away
from narrative. Perhaps we thought, enclosed within the strictures
of a language obsolete for centuries, the triad of the tragedy
was dead and buried, and wouldn't rise again
to prick us from the restless sleep of middle age
and carry us back over the years to the boy who couldn't

surmount his image, to wonder—*finally*—how he had
managed to live, how anyone at all is able to live—
much less like him without a face—through all those years
that stretch ahead completely alone with the self you ruined
and the life you failed to kill.

THE NOISE OF THE JEWS

Townspeople remember that this night was very cold, that the women were utterly exhausted and emaciated, and that they moaned the night away tormented by the persistent cacophony of cries and moans that starving, diseased, wounded, and freezing people make.

—DANIEL GOLDHAGEN, *Hitler's Willing Executioners: Ordinary Germans and the Holocaust*

"The book lay open on a table in the library. So it was an *accident* that I read the passage about how they collapsed in a raped potato field outside a small Bavarian village, and moaned all night on a brief break in the death march. Right away, I realized I had always thought of the suffering of the Jews as a kind of silent movie, the only noise in the soundtrack the harsh syllables of the killers giving orders, the sharp cracks of their bullets. But after reading *that*? I couldn't keep myself from hearing a kind of noise emanating from their poor feet, from their dead hands and torn skin, from their thighs encrusted with nastiness. It was hard enough to *think* about what I'd read. Why did I have to *hear* it, too? I was innocently walking through the library, remember, and there was the book. My eyes fell upon it, and—before I could help it—it had somehow gotten *inside me*! This new horror of the already unbearable horror that my mother always said I thought about more than was healthy . . . You understand, don't you, Mother? I don't *want* to carry their images inside me, or hear them moaning, all night, their soft songs of misery, too weak to raise aloft a volume that could carry their noise to the heavens and rouse The One who was obviously sleeping. *But I just can't help it.* I've *tried* to do as you said: to block it out and go on about my business, and live my life. But now that I've heard it—the noise of the Jews rising like a tune from words on a page—how can I stop listening? How can I silence that icy field? How can I ignore the frosty cursive, glistening like a paragraph in the cold air above the ground, inscribed by the warm groans of barely breathing bodies? My thoughts keep getting hijacked by the music. They run away. They run away and try to lock themselves up inside a cozy, Alpine cottage where a fire on a clean stone hearth crackles noisily, and a fragrant potato soup with sausages swings gently in a pot above the grate, and the soft edges of a hand-bound eiderdown are waiting for me to stuff them in my ears so I hear nothing but the sound of my own thoughts which *should* be delightful in a setting like that, but somehow keep circling back to the frozen field of noise a few meters past the garden gate, and the dissonant music rising from that place, as unwelcome on the ears as a twelve-tone composition in the years before the war when whole audiences of music-lovers walked out on Schoenberg or fist-fought each other in the aisles, not willing to hear what he heard, not able to accept the death of the old harmonies and all that flowed from that, and altered forever the way it was possible for any of us to listen to music ..."

A History of Hair

It was the awful sound of the metal shears
clearing the hair from my wounded head,
cleaving a path for the surgeon's scalpel
that took me back to the bald beauties
of the Holocaust, their pale scalps pitted with scars,
their hairless domes of bony skull.
Extracting that compacted image from a cell
entombed at the center of my mind, I saw again
tons of darkly gleaming hair piling up on the brick floors
of the shearing sheds where the displaced barbers of Stuttgart
and Köln bent above their instruments, preparing to transform
their customers into living images from the canvases
of Edvard Munch and Paul Klee, as if Munch and Klee
realized it all before it had happened, and strove, on behalf
of everyone, to beat back all that was approaching on the inexorable
curve of modern history by sharing the tortured, prescient heads
conceived in their imaginations. As if envisioning, before they were real,
the emaciated eyes of the doomed children of the Jews, or the bodies
of their parents, almost dead, piled haphazardly in a cart
so they almost seemed a trivial cargo of scraped scalps
and laboratory bones, might drain off some of the horror
or shunt it somewhere other than the center of our hearts.

We are carrying this darkness, now, into a second century,
this new millennium with its taste for technology and its fear
of mystery. So when the scissors completed their task, and the razor
was lifted from its metal tray, glinting a little in the harsh light
as if it yearned to be a jewel, and began its airborne journey
towards my head, I knelt inside, as I do at the altar.
There, I make the old gestures to calm myself, and gather
in the air around me the shape of a prayer that might
help me cope. Often, my hands are thrown to my face
in the identical gestures of shame and horror that we recognize
from the works of Munch and Klee. And occasionally, it seems
as if I am not really dying, but actually growing backwards,
devolving to the fetal, returning to that time

when all creatures are closest to God, slick bodies cleaved inside
other bodies, all of us devoid of hair, blind and naked.
A perishing awaits us all, but it is different for some.
Some of us will be shaved and starved down to almost
nothing, and will have to discover exactly what it is like
to be *absolutely nothing*—the abstract shape of a screaming, hairless
head in someone's mind—before we can really begin to live.

SELF-PORTRAIT WITH RELIGION AND POETRY

Sometimes when I write, when Chopin
or Schubert twirls from a disc, when a line
of poetry is perfectly good, the Mystery
is inside me again. I lie down in the silence
of my mind and touch the world all over.
Clouds fly through me. Trees break the sky
above a frozen lake, and a footprint
startles its crust of snow.

Then I can type another page, or nurse
my hungry infant. I can take from the cupboard
the bread and the wine, the eggplant and garlic
my hands will transform into sustenance.

ESCHATOLOGY

And then an awful leisure was—
Our faith to regulate.
　　　—E. DICKINSON

The stone garden she always imagined
cultivating late in life remains buried
in the back lawn. Stones weary her
now with their secrets and their stunned
molecules, with the death they neither
welcome nor avoid trapped inside.
Instead of digging stones, instead of
prying elements up out of the earth,
she follows a chaster plan, rising
each morning at six to brew one cup
of weak coffee lightened with milk.
She drinks it at the window
where the finches feed.

Mornings are reserved for small tasks
and paperwork. At noon, she makes
a cold lunch. A fruit salad
with plain yogurt. Or an open-
face tuna sandwich. She drinks
sixteen ounces of filtered water
and eats an apple without removing
the skin. Then she lies down
in a hot bath, her mind fighting
with the temperature.

Inevitably, the several hours of each
afternoon struggle passionately
with one another, each yearning
to be filled with all that filled them
in the years preceding. She walks
out into the garden but turns away
from the stones sleeping in the unturned sod.

She buries her face in the propped-up peonies,
or in the window boxes bristling over
with thyme. She runs the manual mower
back and forth across the lawn
in every season—anything so she won't
carry herself back to the lusty years
of begetting children, and the decades
of industry that followed.

During the long months of winter,
it's always harder to silence the voices
and dim the images. She often takes
to the sidewalks of our neighborhood,
her tri-pronged cane tapping beside her
in the fallen leaves, or seeking
the solidity of the paving stones
encrusted with snow.

Late afternoons are what she calls
fugue time. That is when she does
three things at once: launders
her clothes in the automatic washer,
and prepares a supper of soup and cheese,
while listening to an English operetta
on a compact disc player strapped
to her waist. Because she no longer cares
for politics or the antics of celebrities,
she stopped following the news and reading
the papers. She canceled the cable. Thus,
her evenings are quiet.

After dinner, there are few dishes
to wash, few lights to turn on. Only
two doors to lock. Then, if she is lucky,
the day will collapse gently in on itself
rather than quaking open, and spilling out free
glimpses of the images she's evaded all day.

She checks the calendar to ascertain
another twenty-four hours has spent itself. Yes.
Now, she can feel it shutting down and losing
power, diminishing to something as compact
and harmless as a stone the size of a bouillon cube,
withering for years at the back of a pantry.
As unconscious as a boulder landscaped
into the design of a garden.

She makes her way up the stairs to her bed
and her book, to the tall clear bottle
with the amber-colored malt resting inside.
Now, her reward will be to lie in bed as mindless
as a stone, herself, gradually reading herself down
into the bland and empty
darknesses of sleep.

SCAR

When the mirror sliced my daughter's thigh,
it slowly flowered open in bloody layers of broken
glass and petaling skin. Now the wound has healed
to a dark, thick worm of keloidal flesh
humped up high on top of her leg. Still,
it destroys me, and the way she walks at the pool
or emerging from the bath—trying to hide
her imperfection with her splayed-out hand—
hurts me the way her puppy's back-end wiggle
signifies a fear of men, and ignites a little narrative
in my mind: some creep with a beer in his hand
batting around a five pound pup, and thinking it's funny.

The fact that I still sneak in like some pervert
to my daughter's bedside and peel back the cover
and lift the gown and hunker down inside a sacred moment
of healed skin and human skill won't be held against me
surely. I pray there, my fingers tracing the raised nub
of once-ruptured skin, my stomach bottoming out,
my mind still raving with the images of that evening, refusing
to relinquish even one detail of the night the Almighty
hung back, masquerading as a dark deity, a complicated god
who would hold a small child hostage and torture her mother.
Now it will take a long time to fasten Him back where He belongs
—the way we falter screwing in a light bulb in the dark, panicked
and visionless, the glass globe turning uselessly in our hand,
the tin rind of the socket refusing to thread, and wondering
what we will see, and who will be there beside us
in the dark when the light finally returns.

THE PSYCHOANALYST'S DAUGHTER

In the quietness of falling snow outside her father's office,
She hears the hushed hiss of passing cars negotiating
Transformed terrain. The muted clank of tire chains.
Skidding carcasses of steel and glass, sliding, uncontrolled
On icy streets. Safe inside, lolling on a chair, its tall back
Hovering above her head, a flaming wave of red,
About to fall and break, she reads. This morning,
Before she left for school, her father, as he always
Does, had combed her hair, and clamped it back
Behind her ears with two neat clips. She still feels
His movements there, his hands separating her frothed-up
Locks into shining, straightened lengths of reddish-brown.
She's ten years old, a colt-like girl her father
Calls "my colt." Her legs two knobbly lengths
Of bony strength, her eyes twin drams of dark, blue depths.
On the other side of an insulated wall, her father's patients
Lie, uneasy, on his aqua-colored couch.
She must know they weep and rail. With wet faces
And bruised fists, they weave their private stories' knotted
Clots of tangled images for him to sort. Just like
Her hair . . . He reads them, like a book, he's said. She loves
To read. Today, the story of a girl who adored her horse
So flagrantly it felt like pain. She laid her head into its butter-
Colored mane and breathed until her whole face flamed
With scent-filled waves of damp horse heat.

Sitting on the side of her canopied bed,
Her father has read to her a hundred books,
Or more. Washed and brushed, warmly buttoned
In the matching halves of her summer
(Or her winter) nightie, she has lain there
Dreamily, inside the tidy boat her small bed makes.
Often, his glasses (the silly, half-there ones he wears
To read) have slipped from his nose and dangled,
Caught, on the chain around his neck
While he has gone on reading, unaware,
And she has gone on listening to the calming
Timbre of his familiar voice. Once, she was alone

Inside her privacy. Now, he's there, but *not* there,
Too: a mystery she loves. Somewhere, Mother
Must be moving busily among her many
Tasks, rubbing cream from the gold-rimmed pot
Into her face, or forking the remains of the evening's
Roast into crumpled foil and placing it, as always,
On the second shelf to chill. But mother's role,
Like weather, has undergone a change. She recedes.
The girl has moored inside her long enough for now.
Somewhere, mother's back there, bobbing in the water
While the girl has swum away. The gritty beach and higher ground
Are what compel her now. She shelters in the covered bed
Her father visits every night, unfailingly ascending
In just this way: book in hand, requesting permission to enter,
Permission to sit. She senses his desire is nothing more
than to sit beside her, reading, quietly, a book she loves.

                                     He touches her
So gently, she sometimes feels a silvery squinch
Of wincing feeling from which she backs away. Like blood
Rising to the surface of a shallow cut and taking on
The shape of pain that hasn't yet begun to throb, she's not
Quite clear what's happening.
                                A horse's brain
Is very small, her father has informed her. And yet
It grows into a creature twelve hands tall, or taller.
Like that, this thing will grow: the germinating
Knowledge he patiently prepares her for.
The day is coming when he'll no longer brush her hair,
Or sit beside her, reading, on the bed, and she'll decline
To raise her hand to trace the curl of gray above his ear.
And neither will she minimize herself to cuddle on his lap
And be embraced by chest and arms. Something grows
Between them that he, so far, protects her from.
Thus far, it is a tiny spark, a wave of fire not yet aflame.
The conflagration that awaits still lies ahead. Its heat
Lies in the story of the horse-adoring girl.

THE WRITER

She has fallen, in the blueish glow of the nightlight,
asleep, her face pressed in the carpet, her hand
still curled around the fat yellow pencil
she has used to write my name on the blank page
of her spiral notebook. Not *Mom,* but *Kate,*
the *K* twirling, vinelike, umbilical, funicular,
down to a nest of scribbles within which
she must have sought the outlines of the four
different letters that compose her name—the name
that is hers alone—for which she alone
must take responsibility—but which she cannot
yet discern within the clamor of her text.

NOTES AND ACKNOWLEDGMENTS

With thanks to Mark Jarman, dear friend and treasured colleague, for reading this book in manuscript and offering suggestions.

I am grateful to: Yaddo, for a residency I enjoyed there in the summer of 2003; the College of Arts and Science at Vanderbilt University, for a very generous sabbatical year that allowed me to complete the work on this book; and the Lannan Foundation, for a Lannan Writers Residency Fellowship in Marfa, Texas, during June 2009.

"A Walk in Victoria's Secret": The Freud quote is from *Introductory Lectures on Psychoanalysis: Lecture XX, The Sexual Life of Human Beings* (1917).

"Sheet: A Psychology" incorporates various quotes (in italics) from William Christenberry taken from various sources on the Internet.

"A History of Hair" is for Gerald Stern.

"The Psychoanalyst's Daughter" is for John Waide and his daughter, Kate.

"The Writer" is for my daughter, Janey Macdonald.

CPSIA information can be obtained
at www.ICGtesting.com
Printed in the USA
BVHW081938300919
559808BV00010B/1422/P